HOW TO REWRITE YOUR STORY

Breaking Free From Self-Limitations

Green Smith

INTRODUCTION

CHAPTER ONE

HOW TO BREAK THROUGH SELF-IMPOSED LIMITATIONS

LIMIT BREAKER

CHAPTER TWO

WHAT IS A LIMITING BELIEF?

WHAT DOES BREAKING LIMITS MEAN?

INSTRUCTIONS TO BREAK YOUR LIMITATIONS

HOW TO MOTIVATE YOURSELF TO KEE BREAKING LIMITS

BREAKING LIMITS INTO SHORT TASKS

BREAKING YOUR LIMITS IN LEARNING

CHAPTER THREE

WHAT QUALIFIES ME?

DEVELOPING YOUR ENTHUSIASM

CHAPTER FOUR

CONCLUSION

HOW TO BREAK THROUHG YOUR OWN LEADERSHIP LIMITS

INTRODUCTION

It is not difficult to trouble yourself with an insight that you can't accomplish something, or you are not adequate. What's more, indeed these discernments can have us caught in a false reality... You start to accept these self-imposed limits. You might feel caught or baffled at being trapped in this cycle. The uplifting news is, that it is feasible to separate free and thump these cutoff points, coming to significantly farther past them.

First we should take a gander at some normal self-limits identified with swimming:

I couldn't say whether I can swim that far

I'm not quick enough

I'm not adequate to share a path

I'm not adequate to swim in untamed water

I'm not adequate to put down that seed time

A new model from the Discovery Aquatics studio was a youthful competitor, getting back to the studio after a break post full iron distance hustling. He had recently made the vocation move from NC to NYC and visits the studio when he is visiting the area. I had the joy of working with him for a couple months, and the most remunerating part of this mentor/competitor relationship, was directing him through delivering himself from his own deliberate restrictions.

After his ironman, swimming took a secondary lounge to work and profession. A fairly ordinary, important life digression. This center had him move to the mind-boggling universe of NYC. He had lost trust in his swimming and in exploring a major city to discover a pool. He had forced on himself that he didn't have the wellness to swim laps, he was not sufficient to share a path, and he would have been the most noticeably awful swimmer in the pool. I could detect the nervousness about this as he talked. Notwithstanding, not really settled to contend in a marathon during spring.

So we conceived an arrangement. It was based around 3 stages to conquering deliberate constraints.

1. Question the limit – who is setting the assumption? At the point when you recognize the cutoff points are being

set from the inside, you can bring the issues out in the open and address them. For this situation, the competitor had talked himself into a bogus reality that he was not adequate. When he perceived this, it was simpler to define an activity plan.

2. Make a rundown – when have you been a triumph? Noticing the occasions you have been extraordinary or fruitful at something will help the mind switch gear. It doesn't need to be sports, it tends to be any time in your life you have progressed nicely. You will rapidly see that you are adequate. For this competitor that rundown was simple – reviewing a few past races and long untamed water swims gave him a pride and moved the outlook to 'I'm sufficient'.

3. Be dynamic in change – make an arrangement. Enroll some assistance to make bit by bit activities, to run after conquering your own insights. For this competitor we started with an exceptionally essential errand. For about fourteen days, the undertaking was basic and sensible. Discover an office to swim, get to the pool and swim an extremely short exercise. This activity was tied in with making schedule, and understanding the truth was not in the least like his made impediments. The input was awesome and he started to see that he was sufficient.

From that point the arrangement extended to 2
deliberate exercises seven days with expanding trouble.

CHAPTER ONE

HOW TO BREAK THROUGH SELF-IMPOSED LIMITATIONS

In my introductions, a message I often share with crowds is "Genuine impediment can be survived; it is the self-imposed handicaps that keep us down." Here's the distinction. A debilitation is substantial and unchangeable, while a willful impediment is fanciful and inconsistent.

Self-imposed limitations your own discriminatory constraint." Self-imposed limits can become incapacities in the event that we permit them to keep us from accomplishing our latent capacity. At the point when an individual draws emotional lines on their ability, they seldom go past them. Here are four rules that can help you get through deliberate limits with responsibility and consistency:

1. Change your own image

Your image is gotten from who you think you are, what others can anticipate from you, and how are you exceptional. Furthermore, a brand has a picture, name, and interior convictions. Perceive that it isn't your ability or abilities keeping you down — yet what you accept about your own image.

As Longfellow noted, "We judge ourselves by what we feel equipped for doing, while others judge us by what we have effectively done." Changing your own image might mean the contrast between acceptable or marvelous accomplishments.

2. Leave the known

Self –imposed limitations cause us to disparage ourselves and overestimate others. Therefore, we will in general remain inside our usual range of familiarity and become hazard safe.

One approach to get through this wellbeing zone is to take a stab at something you have never endeavored. To expand your mental fortitude, center on potential gains rather than potential misfortunes. Keep in mind, only one out of every odd race can be won, yet losing is ensured in the event that you never enter the race.

3. Show some respect

Words can be our most noteworthy resource or responsibility. How we converse with ourselves shapes our viewpoint and can lift us up or wreck us.

Positive language can open additional opportunities, increment inspiration, and be an amazing impetus for defeating nonexistent obstructions. Keep in mind, there will be a lot of individuals that say, "You can't." Make sure that individual isn't you!

4. Play up

As a tennis player, one system to further develop your game is designated "playing up." This implies purposefully playing matches with other people who are further developed.

Have you at any point seen when you ceaselessly rival other people who are less gifted than you, it turns out to be to a lesser extent a test, and harder to stay persuaded to improve? Discover individuals who urge you to accomplish more and be more. This will rouse you to "play up" and push you past your deliberate impediments.

LIMIT BREAKER

You trust you can't talk before a group since you're an introvert. You trust you can't assist with painting a local area wall painting since you're not imaginative. You accept you'll never have achievement since it's only not in your blood.

These things are totally bogus and what's more terrible — some portion of us knows they're false, however it's simpler to clutch restricting convictions like solace covers.

All things considered, it's time we changed that, in this article, I will show you what 'breaking cutoff points' means, how to track down your restricting convictions and a method to help you continue to break those cutoff points so you can at last accomplish what you truly need throughout everyday life.

CHAPTER TWO

WHAT IS A LIMITING BELIEF?

A limiting belief is an idea you have about yourself that you accept to be valid however is really keeping you down. This belief is known as a belief since you believe it.

Here are a couple models:

I can't procure more than X sum, I'm bad with cash

I will not attempt X new thing, I'm not the daring kind

I will not have the option to learn X thing, I'm too old to even consider learning new things

Limiting belief are not pardons, they're things you've accepted for quite a long time since you've been affected to believe them.

At any point had an instructor say you're not learning adequately speedy? I bet you presently accept you're a sluggish student. At any point had a parent call you modest? I bet you presently battle in friendly circumstances. Indeed, even the media can shape how we think and feel about ourselves.

So presently we know what a limiting belief is, we can deal with breaking them.

WHAT DOES BREAKING LIMITS MEAN?

Limiting beliefs don't have a place in your life. In case there's something you need to do or attempt and a limiting belief is keeping you down, then, at that point it's an ideal opportunity to in a real sense break your limit so you can continue ahead with doing it.

Actually like bringing an end to a negative propensity, when you break your limits, you're remembering them, recognizing they exist, and afterward you're dismantling them – breaking them so they presently don't address the restricting convictions you once had.

Sounds complicated, yet we should continue ahead with it, will we?

INSTRUCTIONS TO BREAK YOUR LIMITATIONS

We should do this in a bit by bit measure, so prepare with your first limiting belief.

1. Perceive and recognize your limiting belief

Your limiting belief wasn't made for the time being. The probability is that you've been clutching it for quite a long time. Actually like negative propensities, you're not going to have the option to break your limit a couple of days. It will take some work and self-belief to arrive.

So at this stage, see the truth about your limiting belief, how it arrived and how you feel about it. Record it in the event that it assists you with preparing.

2. Reframe your limiting belief

Since we perceive our limiting belief exists and where it came from. It's an ideal opportunity to move our reasoning. Rethinking your limiting belief essentially implies moving the words you use when you talk about it to become positive.

Here's a model. Rather than 'I can't procure more than X, I'm bad with cash.' You'd shift the words you use to rather say 'I can acquire more than X since I will set aside the effort to put resources into my cash mentality and with training, I can accomplish my objectives.'

The objective here isn't to change your limiting beliefs into absurd articulations which appears to be totally unattainable. A straightforward and sensible change in your outlook is the ideal spot to begin breaking your cutoff points. You can generally go greater down the line.

HOW TO MOTIVATE YOURSELF TO KEE BREAKING LIMITS

So presently we've gone through how to break your limits, it's an ideal opportunity to investigate how to inspire yourself to continue as far as possible.

Breaking a limit doesn't end when you change the manner in which you talk about it. This is the place where it just truly starts. To continue as far as possible, you'll need to begin making a move.

Very much like when we re-outlined our limiting beliefs, we'll need to keep this basic. In the event that you begin intending to make a monstrous move, the probability is, you will not keep it up.

BREAKING LIMITS INTO SHORT TASKS

To truly begin breaking limits, you'll need some speedy successes. So record 4 things that you can do throughout the following week to begin breaking that limit. Make these assignments as little as could really be expected and ensure one of them you can do today.

By separating it this little, the undertakings become significantly more sensible and you'll have the option to see improvement right away.

Here's a model for somebody who needs to begin practicing consistently:

Join the exercise center

Go to the exercise center the following day

Go to the exercise center multiple times that week

Give myself a decent gesture of congratulations

This looks truly senseless, isn't that right? It fundamentally says, join the exercise center and go to the exercise center. Yet, on the off chance that you've been setting caps for this for quite a long time, separating it this little is important to get moving.

This is only multi week of movement. It's not viewing at your cutoff as a gigantic assignment. You're not arranging a month's rec center timetable, you're not choosing which machines to utilize or which activities to do. You're not in any event, pondering the garments you'll wear, and you're trying to say you'll join the exercise center and go to the exercise center. Also, absent a lot of exertion, you're breaking your limits as of now!

On the off chance that you take a gander at your limitations as huge objectives that are way later on, you'll never move towards them.

Presently it's your move, you have your restricting conviction. Compose 4 things you can do throughout the following week to begin breaking it. Separate the errands to considerably more modest ones in the event that you need to, yet don't go longer than seven days. These speedy successes are intended to be fast.

ROUNDUP

With regards to breaking your limits, you're in full control. You can either assume responsibility for them or let them assume responsibility for you. Try not to leave your life alone characterized by the limits you've obtained. Get to remembering them, and afterward get to breaking them.

BREAKING YOUR LIMITS IN LEARNING

In case you are somebody who battles with keeping up inspiration, or on the other hand on the off chance that you end up watching recordings, taking out books, or perusing articles about the most ideal approaches to practice or study, look no further.

CHAPTER THREE
WHAT QUALIFIES ME?

I know the battle. Whatever reservations you have for investing that consistent exertion, or for whatever boundaries you face in keeping up with your inspiration, I have been there. I have a genuine instance of ADD (Attention Deficit Disorder) which keeps me from reliably providing the sufficient degrees of dopamine needed to hold my consideration back from influencing. I have managed the condition as long as I can remember, and I tracked down that not even prescription could affect me. Be that as it may, I generally figured out how to remain useful through somehow. However my capacity to keep focused was variable, there was one thing that consistently took me back to my work and studies... Enthusiasm.

That is incredible. Be that as it may, how can one approach controlling or managing enthusiasm? I have attempted each and every strategy under the moon. I watched inspirational recordings each day. I made frameworks intended to remunerate achievement and rebuff disappointment. I parted with my PC for a whole semester (It worked for a little while, yet I really made myself discouraged by withdrawing myself that way. Also, I'm not a passionate individual!) Every last bit of it gave transitory outcomes with long haul frustration. I'm able to help you since I was at long last ready to figure out how to help myself.

DEVELOPING YOUR ENTHUSIASM

I see a ton of articles talk about "Stream" or "Energy", however that is just one side of the condition. We can speak for quite a long time about how much your Stream can assist you with doing astonishing things, yet ultimately we need to comprehend the best course towards outfitting your Stream when you need to finish that task or start that aspiration. For that, we need to more readily comprehend the progression of dopamine...

So how about we pose a more substantial inquiry. For what reason would you say you are presently perusing this article? The appropriate response is that it offers some benefit, in any case, really recognizing likely worth from the article has more to do with your progression of dopamine once we reclassify what we mean by "esteem". For a few, it could be important just to analyze the article against some others, with no aim of utilizing the data contained in that. For other people, they might be filling a quantity of perusing for the day that offers their benefit to them (And indeed, it could likewise be that you basically discover the words drawing in and anticipate perusing to consummation, and that would be the most immediate type of significant worth that incites the steady delivery and stream of dopamine.) By essentially noticing ourselves in our regular state, we can see that our stream is directed more by what we by and by characterize as important. This leads us to our first conceivable arrangement.

Hack Your Meaning of Significant worth

Would could it be that you esteem the most? Perhaps in case you're perusing this article you're not totally sure of that. Start by taking a gander at the explanation that you're actually perusing. On the off chance that the appropriate response is that you're really hoping to further develop your hard working attitude and learning capacities, then, at that point that is an ideal dispatching point. For what reason would you like to work on these capacities? What might you want to achieve by having the option to learn better or quicker? Is it cutthroat? Would you like to do investigate, ace certain abilities? Whatever the explanation that gives you a base degree of significant worth that is reliable over the long term.

In any case, expansive long haul worth, for example, dominating abilities or building yourself to some aspiring worldview of achievement and satisfaction is momentary at the time, and frequently brings about a dose of dopamine as opposed to a constant stream. This sort of significant worth is more similar to gold in that it is a less liquid item, and more helpful for long term abundance building. What we need is a money that is more liquid than gold, comes in more limited bundles, and permits us to utilize it at whatever point we need it.

Gold is a normally happening asset, actually like our aspirations. In any case, we need to dole out cash that has counterfeit instead of characteristic worth, similarly as nations dole out fake money.

Since we better get it, it very well might be simpler for us to concur that we need to make an incentive for ourselves that depends on however not identical to our inborn qualities. For you as the peruse, possibly the least demanding and most available approach to make this worth is to exploit the drive that drives you to peruse this article. Exploit the way that you need to turn out to be better at learning, and utilize that to make a straightforward framework that feeds esteem into your craving. Award yourself for making strides each day towards the fruition of your characteristic qualities. Reroute your desire towards the means as opposed to the highest point of the step case. How about we examine how.

Make a basic technique to track and progression towards your characteristic qualities. I have made techniques previously, however the best strategies are the easiest. I ought to explain something significant. This strategy will be one of potentially many (contingent upon the person) in a pecking order of balanced governance. This will be your most essential framework to follow the fundamental presence of your proceeded endeavors. Thus, it ought to be your supreme most straightforward technique. Make something similar to a Propensity Tracker, where you check in consistently to report that you finished propensities, for example, "Get Up At 6 AM", or "Check All Propensities" or "Utilize Your Schedule", taking note of for instance that the Schedule is another part to the significant generally framework.

Make a marginally more perplexing technique for unifying your useful conduct. As far as I might be concerned, Google Keep gave an extraordinary method to keep steady over things through a focal association center. I make lasting notes, for example, a "Morning Schedule" where I registration practices that I think would be useful towards getting going the morning great and being getting things done at an early time in the day. I additionally made "Fast Thoughts", "Center Errands", "Composing Thoughts", "Week after week Objectives", "Enormous Objectives", "Understanding

Rundown", "To-Take care of Assignments", and the sky is the limit from there. The fun of utilizing Google Keep is that it gives a phenomenal visual to the entirety of your notes, particularly when you add a significant picture to the highest point of your note to truly make it stick out. Obviously, you can utilize anything as a focal center, like Trello, or some other sort of association space. Simply try to add checking your day by day center point to your fundamental propensity global positioning framework for responsibility!

Make mental connections to other viable frameworks through your focal center. At the point when I made my Morning Schedule note in Google Keep, I tried to add errands, for example, finishing a thing on my Center Jobs, checking the schedule to keep awake to-date on the week, and chipping away at my Daily agenda. That way, this one note goes about as a focal connecting point between three unique frameworks (that aren't too convoluted all alone) so I'm continually mindful of how I ought to do remain useful. Go ahead and execute this procedure in a few regions. It could be goal-oriented to place everything in Morning Schedule in the event that you feel that you will be unable to get up in the first part of the day, so you ought to likewise consider making an Evening Schedule that elements in the chance of early morning disappointment.

Make frameworks intended to arrange and improve on your usefulness.

This can be pretty much as straightforward as keeping an actual note pad in a similar spot each day so you can concentrate all the more viably when the opportunity arrives, or as unpredictable as recognizing and introducing portable or web applications intended to assist you with each undertaking in your framework. For instance, assuming you need to rehearse the piano each day and you're sincerely busy making a melody, you should utilize an application that permits you to save and hear what you have delivered. Or then again perhaps you need to utilize Ever note to follow the entirety of your notes carefully and effectively reference back. Whatever the case, ensure that your framework puts together and makes beginning your undertaking simple and powerful.

Amend at whatever point required. I was extremely glad when I made the framework, however I realized that it wasn't really the end result. Perhaps ultimately I will supplant the whole framework with a basic scratch pad and pencil when I appropriately develop my hard working attitude to where I concentrate better that way. Nonetheless, making counterfeit worth this way first and foremost might be significant for some who have inconvenience and need assistance assembling their hard working attitude now. Having some construction that works and isn't too troublesome makes it enjoyable to follow a framework and become useful. So regardless of whether you have had a terrible involvement in making frameworks for yourself, you should check this out while remembering the significant parts of what we have covered.

All things considered, in case you resemble some who essentially can't depend on a framework to construct their hard working attitude for them, I have guidance for you too. The framework above is just one illustration of numerous potential methodologies, and as a general rule you needn't bother with a framework at all to become useful. Basically recognize your very own approach to hack your Stream and direct your dopamine, and you will have more regular way and comprehension of obtaining inspiration. There are some essential fixings that you should achieve this condition of nirvana.

Recognize Your Motivation

I might be an understudy of math, yet I have a profound faith in God. I accept that God has made everybody of us for a particular explanation. Regardless of whether you are a passionate Christian or a nonbeliever, I figure we can essentially concur that there is an exceptional thing in each one of us that guides us to one way over another. A few group lean towards expressions, others towards technical studies. A few group need to help other people, or educate, or learn, or perform. Despite your calling, we as a whole have one. Your initial step to having steady admittance to your province of Stream is to recognize what you were made to do.

Expect you could learn anything immediately. In case you were set in a room right now by some robot overlord and advised to pick your calling or be annihilated for absence of capacity, how might you decide to help the remainder of your life? You just have a couple of moments to choose. Assuming you can't respond to that inquiry, you have quite recently addressed mine. You don't have anything that propels you, so how is it possible that you would potentially fabricate inspiration or break your cutoff points in learning? You need to discover something that you will battle for. That is your first task.

Assuming you had the option to address that inquiry, you're prepared to continue on to the following stage. When you make certain of how you need to help the remainder of your life, split it up into its more modest pieces. What do you need to learn before you become an expert of your aspirations? What steps do you need to take? What steps would you be able to take at the present time? Become mindful of the stuff to succeed with the goal that you're not debilitate later on. On the off chance that your desire merits battling for, the street ought to be harsh. There was never an effective story that came without difficulty, challenge, or interest. Such a story has no plot. On the off chance that you find that toward the finish of your achievements your story couldn't be told as a legend, then, at that point you need to reconsider your aspirations.

At long last, whenever you have recognized yourself to the guidelines spread out above, you can open your territory of Stream absent considerably more investigation. You ought to just comprehend that your territory of Stream comes when you leave your usual range of familiarity. It comes when you have been upheld to the divider with a cutoff time or a test that really tests the degree of your capacities. It comes when you have something characteristically yours, for example, a task that you need to finish or a cutoff time that you set for yourself, and your capacity is really tried. This is a game. The best gamers on the planet wouldn't be the awesome testing games to push them as far as possible. Give yourself a game that pushes you past your cutoff points. Figure out how to accomplish something you never knew was conceivable. Learning chess? Challenge yourself to overcome each individual from the chess club before the month's end. Learning the guitar? Timetable an exhibition for your companions and book one of them to sing close by you. Figuring out how to paint? Imitate the most well-known piece of craftsmanship from your number one craftsman. These are passages to your province of Stream, and you are ensured to get to it continually once you concede to the test.

Going Up!

The body is made out of muscles and the mind is the same. As you access your territory of Stream to an ever increasing extent, your cerebrum will adjust to the progression of dopamine and direct it all the more reliably. You will track down that the conduits will open and never close. The more you access the express, the simpler it will become to get to it. I'm highly involved with encountering this marvel, as I have never felt as useful as I have for as far back as couple of months. My territory of Stream has worked on additional as I have gotten to it, and think that its superfluous to challenge myself as I needed to in the first place. My psyche normally discovers the test and sets out on the excursion. I don't think, I essentially discover what I need to realize and I learn it.

CHAPTER FOUR

CONCLUSION

HOW TO BREAK THROUHG YOUR OWN LEADERSHIP LIMITS

In leadership—as in all that we do—we as a whole have our own qualities and limits, and the better we comprehend ourselves the more viable we can be. How well do you know your actual initiative potential?

Perhaps you're feeling fixed in by your cutoff points however you don't have the foggiest idea what to do about them. Or then again perhaps you know what you need to do yet aren't sure where to start.

In any case, recollect that we can just change the things we focus on. Change doesn't need to be extreme to be effective, yet even little changes require some work.

In case you're hoping to move past your leadership limits, here are some acceptable beginning stages:

1. Change the focal point through which you see yourself. We will in general consider ourselves to be we generally have, so we judge ourselves on our past and not who we are in the present. In case you're stuck in your own past, update your perspective on yourself and the manner in which you think and talk about yourself. Consider the things you've cultivated and the positive input you've had the opportunity to interface with your potential in the present time and place.

2. Know what you need to change. Individuals who come to me for training some of the time can just say they need a significant redesign. That is not useful or useful. Treat yourself as you would a colleague: your qualities and shortcomings as impartially as could really be expected—possibly with the assistance of a partner or your chief—and focus on the spaces where you most need to improve.

3. Accomplish the work. It's great to know, yet mindfulness benefits you just in case you're willing to invest some work. Getting through your restrictions implies investing energy tending to your conviction frameworks and reevaluating your presumptions. Nothing will occur all alone—arriving at your latent capacity requires difficult work.

4. Recognize and eliminate any hindrances hindering you. We as a whole put impediments in our own way—some we're mindful of and some we can't see. Sorting out your hindrances and attempting to eliminate them is a significant piece of the cycle.

5. Influence your cutoff points. A great many people would advise you to focus on your qualities to arrive at your latent capacity. I have an alternate view. In my book The Administration Hole, I examine the need to use our shortcomings just as our qualities, since what we don't possess winds up claiming us. Realize what you don't progress nicely, what things you consider your shortcomings, and influence those qualities. Interfacing with your maximum capacity implies capitalizing on

everything inside you—your shortcomings just as your gifts.

There are bunches of things you can do to draw nearer to arriving at your latent capacity. Regardless of whether you don't eliminate every one of your cutoff points, understanding yourself is a key to incredible initiative. That is the place where the genuine force lies: in changing what you can, accomplishing the work where it's fundamental, and continually considering yourself a work in progress.

Lead from the inside. As a pioneer, you have power over who you need to be. Do you decide to lead by limits or your latent capacity? Or on the other hand do you work with both? The decision is forever yours.

www.ingramcontent.com/pod-product-compliance
Lightning Source LLC
Chambersburg PA
CBHW051900250726

48659CB00006B/2314